on duty

Life as an Army Demolition Expert

Robert C. Kennedy

HIGH
interest
books

Children's Press
A Division of Grolier Publishing
New York / London / Hong Kong / Sydney
Danbury, Connecticut

Book Design:Michael DeLisio
Contributing Editor: Mark Beyer

Photo Credits: Cover, p. 5, 18 © Indexstock; p. 6, 9, 13, 17, 39 © Leif
Skoogfors/Corbis; p. 10 © David Turnley/Corbis; p. 14, 29, 35 © Corbis; p.21,
22, 25 © Peter Russel; The Military Picture Library/Corbis; p.26, 30, 41 ©
Bettman/Corbis; p. 32 © Steve Raymer/Corbis; p.36 Reuters Newmedia
Inc./Corbis

Visit Children's Press on the Internet at:
http://publishing.grolier.com

Library of Congress Cataloging-in-Publication Data

Kennedy, Robert C.
    Life as an Army demolition expert / by Robert C. Kennedy.
        p. cm. – (On duty)
    Includes bibliographical references and index.
    Summary: Describes the training of an Army demolition expert, including
        information about job duties and a history of explosives used in combat.
    ISBN 0-516-23346-7 (lib. bdg.) – ISBN 0-516-23546-X (pbk.)
        1. Demolition, Military—Juvenile literature. 2. United States. Army—
        Vocational guidance—Juvenile literature. [1. Demolition, Military—
        Vocational guidance. 2.Vocational guidance.] I. Title. II. Series.

UG370.K45 2000
358'.23'092—dc21

                                                                00-027558

CONTENTS

Introduction

Demolition experts are important members of the U.S. Army. These men and women are called Army combat engineers. They plan how to blow up enemy buildings, walls, bridges, and tunnels. Then they carry out their missions using explosive materials and devices. These materials are called demolitions. All branches of military service use demolitions. Demolitions are only used by highly trained experts.

Demolitions include dynamite, TNT, nitroglycerin, gunpowder, and C-4. Each is special in its ability to explode and destroy something. However, all explosives are very dangerous. The Army trains men and women how to use these explosives properly. When used properly, demolitions can help Army units fight. If used

Explosives are just some of the tools used by demolition experts.

improperly, demolitions can cripple or kill. That's why only alert, disciplined people are chosen for combat engineer training. These people must have nerves of steel.

Behind the Nerves of Steel

To handle demolitions, experts must be calm, patient, and careful. They follow specific methods to carry out their work. These methods keep them safe.

WHAT COMBAT ENGINEERS DO

Demolition experts are trained to:

- Disarm and remove enemy mines and booby traps
- Destroy obstacles (barriers), bunkers, and tunnels
- Blast away cliffs, layers of rock, and unsafe bridges to allow fast, new construction
- Create obstacles to slow or stop enemy attacks
- Destroy unexploded shells and bombs, or abandoned ammunition dumps

Mine-detecting machines are used to find mines underground.

HOW COMBAT ENGINEERS ARE CHOSEN

Before enlisting (joining) in the Army, a recruit chooses a career field. Recruits take tests both before and after enlistment. These tests measure their ability to do certain jobs. Before a recruit can become a combat engineer, he or she must score well on specific tests. Then the recruit goes to demolition training school.

Recruits take demolition training at the Engineer School at Fort Leonard Wood, Missouri. The school is a one station unit training (OSUT) operation. Engineers take basic combat training (BCT) and advanced individual training (AIT) at the same time. BCT teaches them how to be soldiers. AIT trains them for special duty.

BASIC COMBAT TRAINING (BCT)

Combat engineers fight as infantry (on foot) soldiers when they are needed. Therefore, they

Recruits are first trained as combat soldiers.

8

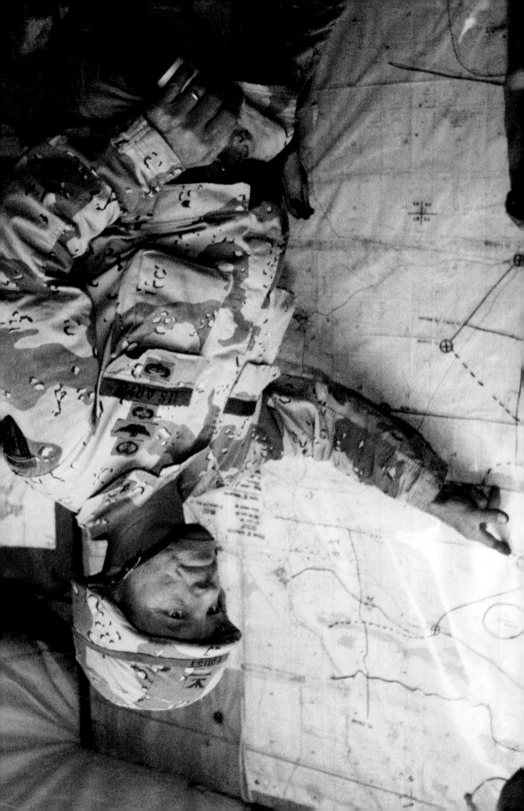

need battle skills to defend themselves and their demolition projects. They gain these skills during BCT. BCT is divided into three phases: soldiering, weapons training, and live-fire training.

Phase One: Soldiering and Common-Task Training (14 days)

This is the most important phase. Trainees learn to properly wear uniforms. They learn to care for their barracks (sleeping area) and equipment. They learn when and where to salute. They learn to work as a team by marching in military formation.

Recruits also learn first aid and map reading. During nuclear, biological, and chemical (NBC) training, they learn methods of contamination (exposure) and possible symptoms (signs of infection). NBC also teaches trainees what to do in case of attack, and how to wear and care for protective clothing.

Another basic skill that recruits learn is map reading.

Recruits train every day. At the end of this phase, they take tests to measure their physical fitness. They are graded on their performances. Afterward, they take part in a ceremony to mark their successful completion of phase one.

Phase Two: Weapons Training (11 days)

This phase focuses on weapons training. Trainees also get more physical conditioning. Good physical conditioning is necessary for survival in battle.

During weapons training, trainees learn how to take apart, reassemble, load, and fire weapons. They must become experts in using all the standard infantry combat weapons. These weapons include:

- M16A2 combat rifle, with M7 bayonet
- M203 grenade launcher
- M249 semiautomatic machine gun
- M60 automatic machine gun

The bayonet is one of the weapons a recruit learns to use.

At the end of this phase, trainees take a physical fitness test. They also take a weapons test. Successful trainees are honored in a special ceremony.

Phase Three: Fire and Maneuver Training (14 days)

This phase stresses self-discipline. By now, trainees know how a soldier acts and what a soldier's goals are. Trainees are expected to focus on tasks and to learn all that they can. Both knowledge and an ability to focus are important because they can mean the difference between life and death to a soldier in combat.

Now trainees receive further weapons and physical conditioning training. This training is geared toward the final tests. Trainees are evaluated on live-fire rifle and grenade ranges, a bayonet assault course, and an obstacle course. On live ranges, real ammunition is used.

Field training teaches recruits what life is like during combat.

Soldiers must be in top physical and mental condition to perform well.

An end-of-cycle test (EOCT), an Army physical fitness test (APFT), and a four-day field training exercise (FTX) judge a recruit's performance during staged combat.

A military ceremony is held at the end of training. All graduates are awarded a weekend pass and are free to leave the post.

ADVANCED INDIVIDUAL TRAINING (AIT)

Recruits training to be combat engineers receive courses in advanced individual training (AIT). Here they learn the job in which they will specialize.

Phase Four: Light Engineer Training (13 days)

Trainees study the basics of demolitions and land mine warfare during the first thirteen

Part of land mine warfare is learning to detect an enemy's buried mines.

Wires connect to the charges that are used to ignite explosives.

days. They have already learned that demolitions include such explosives as dynamite, TNT, and nitroglycerin. These are "high" explosives. High explosives detonate (explode) more quickly, burn hotter, and ignite with much more power than low explosives. Gunpowder is a "low" explosive, which burns, ignites, and detonates more slowly and evenly.

18

High explosives can destroy buildings, bridges, and railroad tracks. They also can be used to blast rock to build a tunnel or widen a river. Combat engineers use each of these explosives for different missions. To know which explosive to use, combat engineers must learn what each explosive is capable of doing.

Trainees learn how to make firing systems to detonate demolitions. There are two types of firing systems: electric and nonelectric. Electric firing systems ignite explosives with an electrical charge. The charge is made with a hand-cranked generator. Once the explosives are wired, a combat engineer

Hidden Dangers

Land mines are explosive devices buried underground. Land mines detonate (explode) when something heavy lands on them. Different amounts of pressure set off different mines. Some mines detonate when a soldier steps on them. Other mines detonate when a truck or tank rolls over them. Combat engineers learn how to place mines. They also learn how to detect enemy mines. To find a mine underground, combat engineers use a metal detector.

turns a lever and an electric charge is sent to the demolitions to detonate. A nonelectric firing system uses a cord (fuse) soaked in a chemical. The fuse is connected to the explosives and is lit. Once lit, the combat engineer must run away before the explosives ignite.

Phase Five: Mechanized Engineer Training (10 days)

During this phase, trainees learn to operate several of the vehicles that help their missions succeed.

The ACE is an armored bulldozer. It protects its driver from enemy gunfire and enemy mines over which the ACE may run. The ACE works the way a normal bulldozer does. It is used to plow trenches, build earth barriers, or move obstacles out of the way.

The M-60 battle tank chassis (frame) is a stripped-down tank that is used to carry a Bailey Bridge. The M-60 tank chassis uses the

The M-60 tank chassis carries the Bailey Bridge.

same engine, frame, and track system as the M-60 tank. However, it does not have a tank turret or cannon attached to it. The Bailey Bridge is a folding bridge. It is loaded onto the back of the M-60 and carried to areas where it is needed. There, the bridge is unloaded from the M-60 and moved into place and unfolded. When unfolded, the Bailey Bridge extends more than sixty feet. The bridge is used to allow tanks, vehicles, and soldiers to cross wide rivers, gullies, and other obstacles.

The armored vehicle-launched bridge (AVLB) is a vehicle that has a bridge attached to it. The AVLB is armored so that it can operate while under enemy fire. Its driver sits in an armored compartment for protection. The AVLB is more flexible than the Bailey Bridge. This is because it doesn't have to have the bridge loaded and unloaded onto its frame. With its bridge already attached, the AVLB needs only to move into place and unfold the bridge. When an

The Armored Vehicle-Launched Bridge uses an attached bridge that unfolds automatically across a river or ravine.

23

Army group completes its crossing, the AVLB can quickly fold its bridge onto itself and get to another location.

Both types of portable bridges are important tools for all branches of the military. Combat engineers must be able to successfully maneuver such vehicles.

To graduate from the AIT, recruits must pass another EOCT, FTX and APFT. Successful graduates are then assigned to a combat company.

Demolition experts learn to maneuver portable bridges.

CHARLES TOW

Historic Demolition Actions

From the American Revolution to Bosnia and Kosovo, combat engineers played a major role in every military action. When a road needed to be built, or a bridge destroyed, combat engineers were called to do the job. The history of combat engineers shows the many different jobs that these important soldiers performed.

AMERICAN REVOLUTION (1776–1781)

An Army engineers group first was formed in 1775. These Army engineers built roads and bridges. They also destroyed roads and bridges to block the British army from advancing. Most of this work was done by hand. Dynamite and TNT were not invented until the nineteenth century. The Army engineers used

Explosives were used during the American Revolution (1776–1781).

gunpowder for blasting. They attached fuses to small kegs of gunpowder that were used to blast away rock.

The Corps of Engineers was established in 1802 by Congress. Its mission was to construct and run the West Point Academy in New York. The Corps motto is "ESSAYONS!" ("Let Us Try!").

WORLD WAR I (1914–1918)

The 11th Engineer Regiment was the first American unit sent to Europe during World War I. These soldiers went to France to clear pathways through German minefields. To find mines, soldiers got on their hands and knees and slowly crawled across a field. As they crawled, they used bayonets to search beneath the ground. When their blades hit metal, they knew they had found a mine. These mines would be flagged for later removal. Finding mines was a very slow process.

Combat engineer units helped to build the trenches in which soldiers fought during World War I (1914–1918).

Demolition experts were sent to find unexploded bombs after the Pearl Harbor attack by the Japanese.

WORLD WAR II (1939–1945)

The Japanese attacked Pearl Harbor, Hawaii, on December 7, 1941. Afterward, explosive ordnance disposal (EOD) teams went to work quickly. There were many unexploded bombs lying on the ground. EOD teams worked to disarm or destroy unexploded bombs and shells at Pearl Harbor. They cleared ships, docks, airplane hangars, and buildings. Afterward, the engineers removed the wreckage.

On June 6, 1944, armies invaded the French beaches of Normandy. The armies were made up of soldiers from the United States, France, Britain, and many other countries. They were known as the Allies. Before they left their ships to board landing craft, demolition experts had worked through the night. Under the cover of darkness, combat engineers attached explosives to obstacles in the shallow water off the beaches. These obstacles included mines, metal barriers, and barbed wire placed by Germans. Before the first landing craft reached those obstacles, the engineers blew them to pieces.

KOREAN WAR (1950–1953)

Clearing mines was a much easier task during the Korean War than during World War I. Army combat engineers now used handheld listening devices. These devices were called mine sweepers. The combat engineers wore headphones. A metal disk on the end of a pole was magnetized. It made a sound for the engineer to hear when it moved over a metal mine. Mine sweeping was still dangerous, but engineers did less crawling on their hands and knees.

VIETNAM WAR (1965–1972)

During the Vietnam War, demolition experts had a huge task. Hundreds of miles of tunnels were dug by the enemy North Vietnamese. Experts say that a North Vietnamese soldier could travel all the way from Hanoi to Saigon (nearly 700 miles!) without leaving the tunnels.

Searching, mapping and destroying the tunnels were jobs for the demolition experts. They dropped into tunnels with flashlights, .45-caliber pistols, and bayonets. They snaked along the muddy floor, measuring distances to turns. They took compass readings. Dragging

Demolition experts had the task of destroying tunnels dug and used by North Vietnamese soldiers during the Vietnam War (1965–1972).

telephone lines behind them, they reported what they saw or did to their buddies above ground. For this dangerous work, the combat engineers gained the name "tunnel rats."

Machines and Tools

Since the end of Vietnam, combat engineers have worked in many places. These places include Grenada (Caribbean), Panama (Central America), and Iraq (Middle East). Each of those operations helped engineers to develop new machines and tools.

ARMORED BULLDOZER

One of the best developments to come out of the Gulf War was the D7G MCAP (armored bulldozer). This bulldozer's cabin is covered with metal armor. The armor protects the engine and driver. This bulldozer pushes mines and unexploded bombs aside to clear a path for troops or vehicles. The mines and bombs are destroyed later by demolition experts.

This bulldozer clears the path for troops and vehicles to cross through mine fields.

Bomb-sniffing dogs are used by demolition experts.

MINE-DETECTING DOGS

Demolition experts are now working in Bosnia (Europe) and other Balkan nations to clear thousands of mines. Modern mines are made of plastic and explosive material. Therefore, metal detectors cannot be used. To find the mines, dogs are used to sniff out the explosives. The dogs smell the explosive materials in the mine.

THE MINIFLAIL

After dogs find the mines, remote-controlled and human-driven vehicles are sent into the mine field. These vehicles detonate the mines. The manned system is an armored vehicle. The operator sits within walls of armor and is fully protected.

The Miniflail is a remote-controlled system connected to an armored tractor. This system uses chains attached to a rotating wheel. Steel arms hold the wheel up and in front of the tractor. When the wheel rotates, the chains are flung against the ground. This causes any mines planted underground to explode.

The importance of this vehicle is that it is remote controlled. No soldiers have to be put in danger to clear mines.

MINEBREAKER

The German Minebreaker 2000 uses speed and impact to destroy mines so quickly that they cannot explode. Here's how the minebreaker works: The huge-toothed blade system is placed on a modified Leopard tank chassis. A spiked cylinder is mounted on the front of the tank chassis. It looks like a garden "rototiller" as it spins and churns up the soil. This blade system spins so fast that it breaks apart and shreds the mine. When the mine is shredded, there is nothing left to explode because its detonator is destroyed.

The Minebreaker 2000 is followed by a tractorlike vehicle pushing a steel strainer. It's called the sifter. Its job is to sift the dirt and catch the pieces of torn-up mines. The bits and pieces are later collected for disposal by demolition experts.

WAR AND PROGRESS

Armies learn a lot about technology by fighting wars. As you've read, mine detection has progressed greatly. Men used to crawl across the

Discovered mines are uncovered for later removal.

ground on their hands and knees using bayonets to probe for mines. Today, there are electronic searching devices and armored mine sweepers to find and destroy the explosives. Demolition experts are always learning new ways to help them perform their jobs safely and successfully.

THE FUTURE OF DEMOLITION EXPERTS

Engineer services are essential. The Corps of Engineers is likely to be around for a long time. Demolitions usually are necessary to complete almost all military missions. That makes the demolition expert's job very secure.

Generals plan attacks by looking at an area of land. They see mountains and gullies, or rivers and plains. Then they order troops to fight through these areas. Engineers plan their jobs differently. They mentally walk the mapped ground that will be the sight of battle. They see every gully and gulch. In a short time, they have planned the bridge that will cross a ravine, or the blast to blow away a rock overhang on a mountain trail. Commanders plan battles, but engineers make those plans work. As long as countries have armies, armies will need engineers.

Planning is a very important phase in all demolition projects.

New Words

Allies group of twenty-six nations that fought against Germany, Japan, and Italy during World War Two

ammunition dump area where explosives and ammunition are stored until needed

barracks a military building housing soldiers

booby trap a hidden explosive device

bunker a protected place used for storage or living

company military unit of two or more platoons

corps military unit of three or more military divisions

enemy territory ground held by enemy troops

infantry ground troops or foot soldiers

mine explosive devise used against ships, tanks, soldiers, and civilians

platoon a small group of soldiers

For Further Reading

Ballard, Joe N., ed. *History of the U.S. Army Corps Engineers.* Upland, PA: DIANE Publishing, 1999.

McDonnell, Janet A. *Supporting the Troops: The United States Army Corps of Engineers in the Persian Gulf War.* Washington, D.C.: United States Government Printing Office, 1996.

Morgan, Arthur Ernest. *Dams and Other Disasters: A Century of the Army Corps of Engineers in Civil Works.* Boston, MA: Porter Sargent Publishers, Incorporated, 1971.

Resources

Regional Recruiting Stations
Midwest
Chicago West Addison Recruiting Station
2550 West Addison Street
Chicago, IL 60618
(773) 327-0070

West
Los Angeles Recruiting Station
1020 South Main Street
Los Angeles, CA 90015
(213) 748-7623

East
New York Lincoln Center Recruiting Station
141 West 72nd Street
New York, NY 10023
(212) 787-0404

South
Oak Cliff Recruiting Station
620 Wynnewood Village
Dallas, TX 75224
(214) 941-1534

Resources

Organization

The Army Historical Foundation
2425 Wilson Boulevard
Arlington, VA 22201
(703) 522-7901
Web site: *www.armyhistoryfnd.org*
This organization is dedicated to educating the public about the importance of the U.S. Army.

Web Sites

DefenseLINK
www.defenselink.mil
This is the official Web site of the U.S. Department of Defense. It includes current news, pictures, and many links to other military Web sites.

Resources

Sapper Leader Course
www.wood.army.mil/sapper
This Web site explains the training that is necessary to become a demolition expert. It includes pictures and a detailed history of the term "sapper."

The United States Army Corps of Engineers Information Network Home Page
www.usace.army.mil
This is the official site of the U.S. Army Corps of Engineers. It includes information on past projects, as well as projects that will happen in the future. Here you can learn more about how the U.S. Army Corps of Engineers helps the public.

Index

Index

About the Author

Robert C. Kennedy entered the U.S. Army at age seventeen and attended various specialized schools. He served with a military intelligence detachment during the Korean War and with a special operations detachment during the Vietnam War, in 1967. He ended his career as an instructor for the Military Intelligence Officer Advanced Course, which he helped to develop, in 1968.